Relationships, Resolutions, and Writing

Relationships, Resolutions, and Writing

Fund-Raising Requests and Applications

Jane Simpson

ISBN-13: 9781981435289
ISBN-10: 198143528X
Library of Congress Control Number: 2017919708
CreateSpace Independent Publishing Platform
North Charleston, South Carolina

Table of Contents

One

Relationships, Resolutions, and Writing

A written fund-raising appeal relies on three factors to succeed: relationships, resolutions, and writing. When a nonprofit organization applies this triad to the organizational mission, it exponentially increases the chances of funding success. The relationship, the resolution, and the writing are of equal importance.

RELATIONSHIPS

- The relationship between the funder and the nonprofit organization can be direct, and the stronger the relationship, the better the outcome.
- The relationship can be indirect. It can be attached to a strong referral from a person who can speak with authority about the organization, the problem, or the resolution. Or it can be based on the reputation of the organization or key leaders. Nonprofit organizations generally have indirect relationships with national foundations or government entities. However, if the relationship is based on a reputation, the applicant must have a stellar reputation.

RESOLUTIONS

- The nonprofit organization offers a resolution to address a specific problem. This resolution represents the consensus of the organization's leaders, the program's leaders, and the participants. The word *resolution* is not to be confused with *solution*, which is a means of solving a problem. Rather, a resolution is a commitment, which implies firm resolve.
- The resolution is a firm decision to address a need.
- The organization offers a verifiable solution to a problem.
- The request for funds to solve the problem generally falls into one of three areas:
  - Programs
  - Capital expenditures
  - Area of the operating budget

WRITING

Writing a proposal or a grant is the simple task of telling the nonprofit organization's story, proving it can accomplish the stated solution, and satisfying the funder that the organization has a long-term purpose. The writer needs specific tools to make the document compelling. The following will give you basic tips for submitting a proposal or a grant that makes a convincing case for a sound organization.

- A well-written request for funds requires the writer's understanding of the program, the funder, the organization, and effective communication tools.
- Begin with an outline of the program and a logic model. Get the necessary approvals.
- Effective writing has authority and authenticity. Keep the sentences simple and the paragraphs concise. Formulate a simple idea, and write a simple sentence. Add another simple sentence, and create a solid paragraph.
- Write in the active voice instead of the passive voice.
- Avoid jargon.
- Clarity is important, and brevity is an advantage. The tone should be straightforward and without flourishes.
- Let the draft rest for three days if possible; then edit it carefully. If time does not permit this, the writer will gain significantly if someone else reviews the draft.
- After completing the request, return to the submission criteria, and review them again. Did the writer include in the first and last paragraphs an actual request for funds with a dollar amount? Did the writer note the number of copies to include and the specific materials to add? Are all the signatures in place? Is the funder's name spelled correctly? Did the writer thank the funder for the funder's consideration?

Two

Researching a Funding Source

Foundations, corporations, and government agencies have dollars to give away. The process by which they decide whom to give these dollars is highly competitive, which makes the writer responsible for learning how to get this money.

Foundations are looking for places to invest their money. The Internal Revenue Service mandates that foundations designate a percentage of their interest-generated income. The fund-raising writer's job is to present evidence that the nonprofit organization receiving these dollars will dispatch them as the donor intends. Moreover, the writer's job is to prove that the organization will provide the funder with a guaranteed return on the investment. The writer must prove that the funder and the nonprofit will be effective in addressing a critical need.

FOUNDATIONS
Explore the available research tools:

- Charity Navigator
  https://www.charitynavigator.org/
- Chronicle of Philanthropy
  https://www.philanthropy.com/
- GuideStar https://www.guidestar.org/
- The Foundation Center
  http://foundationcenter.org/
- The Grantsmanship Center
  https://www.tgci.com/
- The NonProfit Times
  http://www.nptimes.com/

Look for a relationship:

- The IRS gathers information with its 990 forms from the nonprofit about the organization's mission, income, expenses, boards, and programs. The 990s are available from Guidestar and yield relevant information about potential relationships.
- Are there links between the nonprofit board and the foundation board?

Align the organization's resolution with the foundation's mission and stated criteria:

- Is the solution to the problem thorough and proven?
- Is the mission of the nonprofit compatible with the mission or purpose of the funder?
- Can the nonprofit satisfactorily meet the funder's requirements, including those for reports?
- Does the writer know everything there is to know about the source of funds?
- Is it possible for the writer to have a preliminary conversation with the funding organization?
- Do the 990s yield relevant information about past giving patterns?

CORPORATIONS
Look for a relationship:

- Find out whether the business has an internal foundation or whether funding comes from the corporate budget.
- Identify an employee who could speak on the nonprofit's behalf.
- For public companies, look for a board member who could speak on the nonprofit's behalf.

Align the organization's resolution with the corporate giving policy:

- Corporations have stated policies and the writer must examine their guidelines carefully.
- Corporations view philanthropy as marketing opportunities. Working with a nonprofit can help a corporation improve its brand.

GOVERNMENTS
Look for a relationship:

- Identify the regional offices of federal agencies, which might be an invaluable source of help.
- Attend all review sessions.
- Call the contact person; organize the nonprofit's plans, and if possible, meet with the contact.

Align the organization's resolution with government agencies' requests for proposal (RFPs):

- Will the nonprofit follow the guidelines exactly?
- Will the nonprofit read the regulations thoroughly and repeatedly?
- Can the nonprofit organization deliver on the proposed use of funds?
- Can the nonprofit provide meticulous and accurate reports?
- Does the nonprofit have access to matching grant money?
- Does the nonprofit have strong leadership to execute the grant?
- Can the organization provide documentation of need?
- Are the needs compatible with funding guidelines and trends?
- Can the nonprofit prove it can sustain the initiative at the conclusion of the award?

Three

Preparing to Write

Funders request different kinds of documentation about the nonprofit organization. The following is useful information to have readily available:

- The Internal Revenue Service 501(c)(3) letter
- Board of directors list
- Organizational budget
- Audit
- Previous donors list
- Annual report
- Resumes of program directors

Often, the person writing the request is unfamiliar with the technical aspects of the resolution. This unfamiliarity is an advantage; funders, in many instances, are not proficient in complex details and technical jargon. Also, the strongest proposals are those constructed as a team effort. The writer has to work closely with responsible leaders of the program and may at times have to nudge, prod, or cajole them into providing and reviewing information. However, the burden of responsibility to determine whether the resolution has any potential weaknesses rests on the writer. The writer must ensure the program is sustainable and affordable. Funders prefer to see their resources benefit a great many people. They do not want to fund a program that will disappear once the funding cycle ends. They also do not want to duplicate programs unnecessarily, nor do they want their funds going to a program that has previously failed somewhere else. Foundations and corporations do not want to cover costs that government sources will cover. Moreover, in the social service sector, funders are not inclined to fund programs for people who could afford to pay for them. The arts and education programs and projects are exceptions.

The writer has two focuses: to sell the organization and to sell the program. Be careful to consider what information the funder is requesting. When the request asks for a budget, consider whether the budget is for the program or the organization. Does the organization's material on leadership include information on those who will manage the program?

Before sitting down to write a request, consider the following:

- Can the nonprofit organization achieve the stated purpose of the program?
- Does the nonprofit have the proper resources to manage the program?
- Is the organization pursuing the program or the money?
- Has the writer addressed the weaknesses of the organization and the program?
- Has the writer proposed how the organization will overcome these weaknesses?
- Can the writer meet the deadline?
- Is the writer submitting a good proposal for a bad idea now or a good proposal for a good idea later?

Note that the writer reserves the right not to submit.

Some novice writers believe that submitting brochures, pamphlets, photos, expensive binding, and page tabs help sell the request. Sadly, it's not that easy, and sometimes unnecessary attachments can hurt a request. There are ways to organize a request, however, that help convey a professional, competent organization. If the request is a written attachment, not an electronic application, use bold headings and subheadings. Label supporting documents. Provide complete, concise responses. Always repeat the question. For example:

What is the mission of the nonprofit organization?
The mission of ______________ is to ______________________________

Many funders are reluctant or unavailable to speak with a nonprofit organization before the organization submits a request. Sometimes, however, it is possible to have an information meeting, and many potential funders encourage it. Communicate (via phone or e-mail) with the potential funder to learn whether the nonprofit can set up a meeting. Include in the call or e-mail the types of questions the nonprofit seeks answers to so if a meeting is not possible, the funder may answer them at that time.

Four

Developing a Plan

Planning is a comprehensive examination of the proposed program and requires the participation of leaders from throughout the organization, including senior level and program management level. A preliminary plan will help ensure the program is sound. The program plan is not the long-range plan for the organization. Rather, it is a distinct component of the long-range plan that complements the organization's mission, goals, and long-term agenda. The greatest advantage of a program plan is that the planning partners within the organization can spot areas of weakness.

The plan highlights available resources from the community, other existing services, the organization site, equipment, personnel, continuation funding, additional funding, staff qualifications, board involvement, and numbers of volunteers. Moreover, the plan describes potential needs and their costs, including those related to the program site, personnel, equipment, training, and evaluations. The plan indicates whether the timelines of the initiative and the funder are compatible. It also indicates whether the evaluation aligns with the organization's mission, purpose, objectives, and budget. And it clarifies to the organization the probability of short-term outcomes and long-term impacts.

LOGIC MODELS

A logic model shows the processes the organization will use to execute a successful program; it does this by assessing all the available information. The logic model is a tool to assess programs and align the program activities with the organization's mission. It's an excellent resource for a new program and is as useful to the organization as it is to the funder.

A logic model is a planning document whereby the program planner can connect on paper the program's assumptions, resources, activities, outputs, and outcomes. The logic model establishes from the outset how the program will move from concept to effective implementation, and it addresses how critical measures of performance can be identified.

Logic Model	
Problem	A critical need within the nonprofit organization. The logic model proposes ways to change this problem and provides evidence that the solution is viable.
Resources	A description of the assets on hand that will support the solution to the problem. These assets include dedicated space, equipment, materials, time, personnel, board support, personal relationships, sustainability, and plans for the future.
Activities	The proposed solution to a critical need or problem based on a series of predetermined changes, enhancements, and actions.
Outputs	A description of the expected evidence-based achievements based on the implementation of the solution.
Outcomes	A description of the short-term (one- to three-year) expectations of the changes that will result from the solution.
Impact	A description of the long-term (three-years and longer) expectations of the changes that will result from the solution.

Five

Approaching the Funder

The submitted request must comply with the format specified by the funder. It could be in one of the following formats or a combination of these formats:

- Online application
- Executive summary
- Cover letter to attached request
- Letter proposal
- Letter of intent/interest/inquiry (LOI), to be followed by a full proposal if requested
- Full proposal

ONLINE APPLICATION

For online applications, follow this tried-and-true method: prepare the organization's response in a document, and save it on a hard drive before attempting to fill out the online application. Doing so guarantees access to spell-check and word count. It also ensures that the information is not lost if the online application doesn't save or transmit. In most cases, online applications allocate space for an exact number of characters or words to questions, which means every word is relevant.

EXECUTIVE SUMMARY

The executive summary is one to two pages that convey a succinct description of the relevant information, without all the details. Often, in those instances where the nonprofit has an established relationship with a foundation or corporation, the executive summary is the preferred method of communication. Rather than assume the risk of a judgment call, ask the funder's contact person to clarify what the funder expects. Indicate the title of the program, and state that the organization is a 501(c)(3) nonprofit. Address the organization's need, resolution, purpose, objectives, capacity to change the problem (history, credentials, and subject matter expertise), and ability to sustain the program once the funds are spent.

COVER LETTER TO ATTACHED REQUEST

The cover letter must be simple and, at best, one page. It should be on the organization's letterhead and signed by the highest-ranking official within the organization. In some instances, there might be two signatories, including the chair of the board of trustees and the leading executive of the nonprofit. The cover letter should also give the name of the contact person who can best answer questions about the proposal. Include the amount of the request. Show how the nonprofit organization and the funder have similar priorities. Indicate the title of the program, and state that the organization is a 501(c)(3) nonprofit.

LETTER PROPOSAL

A proposal that is a letter begins with the salutation, includes the details of the full proposal, and concludes with signatures. In this instance, attachments help establish organizational credibility and additional information.

LETTER OF INTENT/INTEREST/INQUIRY

Writers are sometimes asked to submit an LOI, which some refer to as a letter of intent and others consider a letter of interest or inquiry. For the purposes of fund-raising, it's all the same. The LOI is a one- to two-page document, unless otherwise indicated, that gives the funder a broad outline of the program for which the writer is soliciting funds. Funders will specify what they want to see in the letter. A strong LOI is based on the logic model and includes the purpose and objectives of the program. Should the funder indicate an interest in the program by requesting a full proposal, the writer will flesh out the details that the LOI outlines. The LOI is similar to a cover letter, but it is more comprehensive. The following are the basics for constructing an LOI:

- The LOI is a business letter written on the organization's letterhead. Do not minimize the importance of relationships: Address the letter to the appropriate individuals, and sign the letter with the name of the highest-ranking leader within the organization. Use the signature as an opportunity; if a board member knows the funder, include that board member as a signer of the letter.
- Open with a sentence that states the organization's name, the funder's name, the name of the program, and the amount the organization is seeking.
- Introduce the organization, and summarize details that establish credibility. This is the place to cite recognition, notable successes, leadership skills, longevity, and other organizational strengths. Align the mission of the organization with that of the funder.
- Document the need and how it relates to the community. Give details about the audience that will be served; include specific demographic details.
- Describe the program with specific details, including the organization's capacity to accomplish these activities. List the qualifications of the staff who will manage the program, and include any site or equipment assets that will support the program.

- List the goals and objectives, which are based on the critical need.
- Identify the process of evaluating the program based on whether the organization successfully achieves the stated goals and objectives.
- Address funding at all levels, including the organization's overall fund-raising success, other funding already secured to cover a portion of the program costs, other funders to be solicited, and plans to sustain funding in the future.
- Close with courtesy.
- If allowed, include attachments that strengthen your request for consideration.

FULL PROPOSAL

The full proposal presents detailed, current, and accurate information and includes the following:

- Introduction and summary
- History
- Need
- Purpose and objectives
- Activities
- Budget
- Management
- Evaluation
- Supporting documents

The next chapter offers a detailed description of the information necessary to include in various approaches to a funder. Although the amount of space varies in the different approaches, the salient facts remain the same.

Six

Writing the Proposal

The writer must honestly and succinctly prove three claims in a request for funding:

- The organization is strong and capable.
- There is a critical problem/need.
- The organization has a credible solution.

The following is an organized tool to prove these claims:

1. **Introduction and summary**
   Provide a brief overview of both the organization and the program.

2. **History**
   The history should be brief, with highlights of key dates. In those instances where space is limited, refer the funder to an annual report or other materials that include a more detailed background. Use the history section of the request to establish long-term commitment to the mission and from the board and staff. Finally, use the history section as an opportunity to highlight the organization's effectiveness within the community.

3. **Need**
   The need must meet three requirements:

   1. It must align with the organization's purpose and objectives.
   2. It must relate to those served.
   3. It must relate to the funder's priorities.

   The organization must be able to document the need. This documentation should include narrative and statistical information. Make sure the information is current and relevant. Do not include copious amounts of industry-related data that is mind-numbing and incomprehensible. The following are examples of resources to demonstrate need:

- Waiting lists
- Survey results
- Census reports
- Legislative committee reports
- Public hearing testimony
- Area Regional Commission information
- News articles

4. Purpose and objectives

The nonprofit organization must present a viable solution to the critical need. Together, the purpose and objectives should convey the benefits of the program to individuals, families, groups, institutions, the community, and the funder. This section is an opportunity to delineate concrete details of the proposed solution—that is, why it will work.

The purpose is a broad statement expressed in the narrative form, and it tells the expected achievements or benefits of the proposed solution. The objectives express the program strategies in terms of expectations and identifiable results. The request aligns the activities and the measurements to each objective, but a request with a lot of objectives can become unwieldy. It is reasonable and practical to list three to four objectives for a program. An objective is an action with a measurable result; therefore, always begin the objective statement with an active verb:

- To increase…
- To decrease…

5. Activities

The activities, or methods, should be consistent with the objectives. This section is an opportunity to begin the detailed justification of the proposed solution: the methods that will make it work, make it different from other recommendations, and make it succeed in the future. Include a detailed description of the methodology. The activities section should include information about the facilities, participating staff, program equipment, and any other contributing factors. An especially valuable asset is an involved board; a description of board involvement can be used to demonstrate the potential for long-term support of the program.

In this section, the writer also gives start and end dates for the application of the funds to the program. The timeline is a critical organizational tool and should be carefully constructed, based on realistic projections. While most funders allow wiggle room in a timeline, an experienced writer will allow ample time for these adjustments. There are many methods of indicating time frames as they relate to the program. The following are just two examples:

I. Narrative timeline

Thirty days from funding…
Sixty days from funding…
Ninety days from funding…

II. Gantt chart timeline

Month	1	2	3	4	5	6	7	8	9	10	11	12
Get bids	■	■										
Recruit staff		■	■									
Sign contracts			■									
Hire staff			■	■								

6. Budget

The most important information about the budget involves the math. Make sure the budget adds up and the math in all instances is correct. Also, funders are more inclined to fund an initiative that serves many people; do the math to determine the projected per-person costs. A writer new to the business of requesting funds needs to recognize the distinctions between the budget of the organization and the budget of the program. Ultimately, the request will include both budgets; however, the writer should pay close attention to the placement.

The budget has two parts: (1) an itemized cost sheet and (2) a brief narrative description of the costs. Always include the word *Projected* in the budget title. Be realistic when projecting the budget, neither padding nor undervaluing the costs.

Costs may be considered direct or indirect. Direct costs are specific expenses of the program, and indirect costs are expenses of the organization as a whole. Very few funders consider indirect costs, so the writer should check with the funder before including them in the budget.

Finally, plans change. In situations where there are major differences between the budget submitted and the actual use of funds, it is the responsibility of the organization to notify the funder in writing for approval to make these changes.

7. Management

The management section highlights the organizational leadership, and the program leadership if they are distinct. When describing the management, the writer focuses on the board and the staff. Describe the structure and characteristics of the nonprofit, and maintain a current organization chart to include if asked. Include information in the narrative about the experience and qualification of the program administrators, and if the funds will be used for new hires, include job descriptions.

8. Evaluation

The evaluation consists of metrics that complement each objective and demonstrate the success of the program. The writer already has delineated the evaluation in the logic model and in the action verbs in the objectives. The evaluation actually begins at the onset of the initiative. For an enhancement to an existing program, the writer establishes a baseline to show evidence of change. For a new initiative, the metrics will prove how the change brought about by the program addresses the problem. The evaluation results will be summarized at the conclusion of the initiative and reported to the funder. It is important to conduct ongoing assessments, because not all evaluation results are positive. It is a testament to the integrity of the organization to include these metrics in the report. The funder understands that complications arise to even the best plans. What is important to the funder is how you address the information and move the data in the desired direction.

A strong request includes quantitative and qualitative information. Quantitative documentation relates to quantity—for example, statistical documentation that includes numbers. Qualitative documentation relates to quality—for example, anecdotal information presented in a narrative form. The following are examples of evaluation tools:

- Baseline data (quantitative)
- Pre- and posttesting (quantitative or qualitative)
- Statistical evidence (quantitative)
- Interviews (qualitative)

The evaluation results will also support the assertion that the program can sustain itself. The writer should highlight how the program's success will have a long-term community impact, and should demonstrate how the organization will continue to fund the project, if it is an ongoing expense. The funder wants to see evidence of interest or commitments from other sources.

9. Supporting documents

The supporting documents are included as attachments, or appendices if the funder allows. The writer should be selective and include only what is relevant. If the funder requests a letter of support, write a draft of the letter that includes details relevant to the initiative and send to the signatory.

The following are examples of supporting documents:

- 501(c)(3) tax-exempt letter
- Annual report
- Financial audits
- Organizational budget
- Media items
- Brochures
- Staff bios

Seven

Following Up

FOLLOWING THE SUBMISSION

After submitting the request, the nonprofit organization sits back and waits. Occasionally the nonprofit may have a reason to send an attachment to the proposal, but the reason has to be a good one. For example, if the organization receives a prestigious award that adds to its credibility, send it as an information piece requiring no response. Update the request if there are major changes to the initiative or the organization, including changes in key personnel.

WHEN A REQUEST IS ACCEPTED

If the funder accepts the request, send a thank-you note and a report on the use of funds at the conclusion of the timeline. The requesting organization can research the funder's giving patterns in the 990s and the foundation directory to determine how soon it can reapply. Finally, if the funded initiative generates publicity, notify the funder. It is critical, above all, to maintain a relationship with the funder in interactions that do not include requests for money.

WHEN A REQUEST IS DENIED

If the funder denies the request, send a thank-you note. Sometimes (but not often) in this case, a potential funder will indicate weak areas and advise on applying again in the future.

The above information provides general guidelines, and these guidelines are not absolutes. The writer should use common sense. Moreover, a fund-raising request that rests on the relationship-resolution-writing triad increases the well-being of the nonprofit in terms of funding, delivery of services, and demonstration of commitment to the community.